# Becoming a Writer

# Becoming a Writer

By David Kherdian

CASCADE PRESS

Cover illustration by Lusine Ghukasyan



Published by Cascade Press
under exclusive license from David Kherdian.

Kherdian, David. Becoming a Writer
Summary: David Kherdian delves deeply into his past as he details the friendships, experiences, and places in time that led to his becoming a writer.

ISBN paperback 978-1-948730-93-8
ISBN hardcover 978-1-948730-94-5

Inquiries regarding permissions or bulk printing requests should be sent to info@cascade.press

For the latest updates and news about publications, be sure to sign up for our newsletter at www.cascade.press

FOR THE KAISERLIANS
Who helped me to see light at the end of the tunnel
this book is belatedly dedicated

Vartine
Lucy
Hart
Mary
Mikey
Maggie
Sot
Gob
Allie
Ardie

# *Contents*

# Our Neighborhood

In a not so small Midwestern town like Racine each separate neighborhood transforms itself into a miniature village that becomes known to itself, while at the same time lending its protected identity to the city that shelters it. It is from here that its storied life begins. Midwesterners have always seen themselves as insignificant players in the unfolding drama of our nation. It is for this reason that its neighborhoods have taken on an exaggerated importance in the lives of its inhabitants, and why each of them finds it necessary to make their own heroes and myths, their national heroes seemingly too far away to be truly believable.

It is from this private, insular world, the world of my own neighborhood, that I entered life, and where, both alone and with all the others, I began to explore the streets and bridges and man-made structures of this, our place, that is also defined in large part by our great lake and the winding river that lent us its name. These were the waters that anointed us by supporting the life of the city and all its neighborhoods, and this is where our growing family met—on the beaches and piers of Lake Michigan, and along the wandering river banks of Root River, with its pavilions, benches, bubblers, and open parks.

Neighborhoods, for children at least, are determined by the young players themselves, their daytime adventures, and nighttime games, that in our neighborhood included the raiding of gardens, stealing custard from the cans left to cool at night behind Kummel Bakery on State Street, while all the while making sling shots, repairing inner tubes to inflate and take to the beach, building shoe shine boxes, with which to roam the night-time streets, shyly entering taverns with a neighborhood buddy, that for me was either Howie Sell or Lotch Oglanian, our price for a shine: one thin dime.

We stayed close to home when we raided gardens, since these were the neighborhood gardens familiar to us. Tomatoes and spuds were our favorites to raid, and often we would meet up at Hansen's backyard, where a bonfire would be in progress, to which we would contribute our spuds. Butsey Hansen or Bill Zaehler, Jr. would play their harmonicas, while we sang a Western hillbilly song, or just howled at the moon, enjoying our plunder and petty crime, our comradeship making us feel special because we were, willy-nilly, making our own little mark in time.

My street was Superior Street, linked by a broken chain to five additional streets bearing that name. Our Superior Street seemed to end at our own dead end block, but I learned later that it had in fact continued, not forward from the base of our dead end street, but instead several blocks further on, where it began acquiring additional segments.

Our block long Superior Street had begun at State Street, which was the street that divided North from South in Racine, and served as one of the boundary lines of our neighborhood, along with Liberty Street one block below State, that ran from Superior Street to the Northwestern Railroad Station, whose tracks demarked the western boundary line to Prospect Street, where began the interrupted northern boundary, connecting itself to Jackson Street, which began at La Salle Street, and ended at Douglas Avenue.

Our home on Superior Street was the second to last house at the end of the block, but for us dead end meant only the secession of vehicular traffic, because of the rickety wooden stairway that led below to a barren dirt courtyard bordered on each side by one and two story factories, before opening onto Prospect Street and our expanding neighborhood beyond. Facing the last six or seven homes on our Superior Street block was an abandoned factory attached to Porter's furniture repair shop, where our neighbor, Dickie Steberl worked and learned the carpenter trade.

The noises from all these factories didn't annoy us, because by now the raucous music of the many industries around town had become a constant erratic background music in our lives, not to mention the smells, particularly Wink Soap Company on West Street, and from there all the way to the tannery beside Root River on 6th Street. The city had long ago accepted these sounds and smells as an irrefutable condition of its life, because these were the work places where most of our fathers spent their unending years of hard labor.

Just below our block, on Prospect Street, was

our own neighborhood blacksmith shop, a miniature factory of its own, set back from but opening onto Prospect Street, and although noisy, it was not as loud and angry sounding as the foundries and factories, with their frequently opened doorways, inviting us to come look inside as passive participants of its fiery contents and sweltering heat, where we could watch the busy, sweaty workers toiling inside.

The home of our next door neighbors, the Zaehlers, was not ten feet distance from our own, housing Bill, his wife, Clara, and their two children, Bill, Jr., who was older than me, as his sister Deanna was younger, although she in turn was older than my kid sister, Virginia. Uncle Bill, as he was known to us, worked in a print shop in Chicago, a part-time fisherman who poled his nets out to dry in his backyard, which ran parallel to our own, meeting at the terminal point of the Hansen's backyard, who were his relatives. Our yard connected us to the Giragosians, whose two story house contained their grocery store, fronting on La Salle Street, a grocery store that would come to play a crucial role in the life of our neighborhood.

Our backyard was full of my father's many growing plants, contrasting dramatically with our neighbor's on either side. My father had come from a family of peasant farmers in Adana, Turkey, that we called the Homeland because we were Armenians, not Turks. This was after the Massacres, that both my mother and father had survived. Our grape arbor, built by the German family who owned the house before us, became the entryway to our yard, where my mother visited at times with her friends, and where I cleaned the fish I caught, and later dressed the wild game I had bagged in Scouts Woods. My kid sister had her birthday parties there, although her favorite place in our yard was the swing we had made for her in the plum tree. Our tidy vegetable growing garden was divided by a wooden fence from the trafficked, weedless Zaehler yard, with its junk autos, nets poled out or stacked against our fence, with a broken down shack in back on our property, that had once been a garage, but became a rental at fifty cents a month for Bill and his minnow and crab tanks.

The homes of the Giragosians and Hansens were fronted on La Salle Street. To get there I would usually pass through Zaehler's backyard, which was the common thoroughfare for anyone living on our block. When not using Zaehler's yard, I went through the Giragosian yard, where a separating mulberry tree stood, separating our properties. In season I would stop and eat the toots, (Armenian for mulberry), which I thought of as our own fruit because of its popularity in the homeland.

Next door to the Giragosian's lived the Webers, whose chestnut tree grew majestically atop their raised lawn, that we raided every fall without needing to ask permission. We waited for the first cold snap of winter, causing the withering leaves to fall, exposing their chestnut bounty to our eyes.

Just across the street was a narrow brick-lined passageway named Gideon Court, a T-shaped enclave of individual houses that permitted foot and bicycle travel only. It was a strangely attractive anomaly, holding a special appeal for us, in part because we were unable to name what that feeling was. We must have thought of it as eccentric, in part because the people that lived there always struck us as odd, in particular the one Armenian family that lived among the six or seven houses on that plot, they being clearly the oddest Armenian family in our community, and so it seemed fitting that they had found this setting for themselves.

Gideon Court, when entered from La Salle Street, exited onto Marquette Street, a short block away, with Gideon Court morphing into West Street—going from red brick to everyday asphalt. Just beyond the corner house on West Street, there were a string of apartment-like dwellings, running perpendicularly from front to back. The next house on that block was uniquely situated to face the first of these apartments, with a windowless basement, opened at one end, where a makeshift door led into its secret, darkened quarters. Dwelling there, alone and forsaken, lived Crazy Eli, as he was known to adults, but named by us, Kookoolala. The sunken hollow that led to his "home" was clearly off limits, because he was the only bona fide madman in our neighborhood. The next structure on West Street, a two story brick building had its entrance on Geneva Street, housing a bakery run by an Armenian man who sometimes gave us day old sweet rolls on our way to or from school.

Turning left from there, a short block away, stood Garfield School where Geneva Street had T'd with Milwaukee Avenue. On our return home from Garfield at the end of the school day, we often played marbles, which consisted of taking turns with one marble chasing another until the thrown marble struck the other marble, to then be turned over to the victor. Should one of our marbles tumble off the sidewalk and enter Kookoolala's forbidden dirt cavity entryway, we would be forced to leave it behind. Staring down at our abandoned marble, we'd remain motionless, until other classmates showed up, when, gathering courage as a group, we would begin shouting down loudly, "Kookoolala is kookoo, Kookoolala is kookoo," until at once he would burst out from his door, charging after us with an axe flaying over his head, grunting and bellowing in a crazed mixture of guttural sounds that terrified us as much as his axe, as we ran with frenzied and terrified excitement in all directions.

Beside Garfield School stood an old ramshackle storefront that had been an Armenian Coffee House during my early school years, inhabited by refugees of the Massacres, who gathered there to share their sorrows, play backgammon and drink Turkish coffee.

Rognerud's filling station was next door, at the corner of State Street. Across the street, and just around the corner from there, at Marquette and State, stood our one and only neighborhood drug store, owned by and named after Mr. Derse himself, our friendly, purveyor of drugs and comics, with a horseshoe soda fountain in back, where for a quarter we could sit down and have a malted milk shake, with soda crackers on the side. Horlick's plant for the making of malt was one of the more famous industries in our town. Across the street, also on the corner of State and Marquette stood the Thomas Hotel, and next door Dadian's shoe repair shop that was squeezed between the Thomas Hotel and Dania Hall, which was once the hub of the Danish population, who were the first settlers of our neighborhood, but who were long gone to the faraway West Side, leaving their hall behind for rentals, and with their church, just two blocks away, now the property of the Armenians, who had renamed it St. Mesrob's Armenian Apostolic Church.

Crossing Marquette Street from Derse's, onto State Street, the first storefront was Houman's Fish Market, with fresh catches always on display in their storefront window, sitting invitingly on crushed ice. Next door was Rice's Bicycle Shop, and further down the street the State Street Hardware Store that kept its bamboo fishing poles in a circular tube on the sidewalk for their customers to test before making a final selection. One block further, after crossing La Salle Street, came Superior Street, with the cavernous Public Fruit Market opening onto both streets, where everyone in the neighborhood shopped for fruits and vegetables. Huron Street came next, and then Douglas Avenue, a main thoroughfare, that began at that corner, running north all the way out of town. Our own neighborhood stopped just two blocks from there on Jackson Street—one block beyond Prospect Street—Jackson's lone block ending at La Salle Street, thus completing the jagged rectangular boundary of our neighborhood. Lotch Oglanian lived on this block, as did Dick Kizewic, the Kaprelians, and Larry Bekken, all of whom had a place in my life and later in my work.

At the corner of State and Douglas Avenue stood the J. I. Case office building, and across the street its factory, the industrial giant of our town along with Johnson's Wax. The long first block of Douglas Avenue, before it reached Prospect Street, was the home of numerous businesses. Nearest the corner, Charlie Margosian's tavern, that catered to African-Americans, with a similar tavern next door, occupying a building that had once been the Massis Hotel, named after Mt. Ararat's straddling sister mountain in far off Armenia. Also on this block an Armenian coffee house that Lotch and I would enter with our shoe shine boxes, and after much questioning and pandering we'd be assigned to a customer, finally departing, if we were lucky, with a half dollar between us.

As children we often walked this long first block on Douglas Avenue, from State Street to Prospect Street, but it never really touched us, as did all the other streets in our neighborhood, probably because it catered to the needs of adults, not us. But there were other reasons as well, that were hard to put our finger on, having to do with its emotional remoteness, not only because of its people, but because it was barren of trees and grass. State Street, seemed to fit our shoes and swagger best, as we sauntered past all the doorways and vacant lots, feeling at home among familiar neighbors.

Following its own jagged line, our neighborhood's eastern perimeter became the Pugh's Coal office, corner of Ontario and State; from here, we turned off State Street to walk through the coal yards bordering Root River, with its row of factories on the right, ending at the condemned bridge just below the YMCA, our usual destination, that bridge being both our neighborhood boundary line and our shortcut to downtown. It was our world, that we alone traveled, a shortcut that took us past the coal yards along the winding river, until we reached the rickety wooden bridge, that we crossed to enter the city lights, that were initiating us into its grown-up life. This would be our pathway to the movies and the YMCA, also the Park Arcade, with its pinball machines downstairs, and the Ace Grill, where we shot pool, before returning home in the dark, back over our bridge, listening for the drop forge hammer to resound and send an orange glow into the night sky.

Opposite Ontario Street and the coal yards, Erie Street continued the line of the eastern perimeter of our neighborhood, the first long block ending at Umbaji Park, our name for Colbert Park, that was also once known as Bum's Park, but named by us after the old, forlorn Armenian man who seemed to have made it his home, occupying always the one lone bench that sat at the top of the lawn, that we'd pass on our way to Lake Michigan, stopping to quench our thirst at the bubbler located at the bottom of the tiny triangular park.

As we got into our teenage years, our interest in food revolved exclusively around hamburgers, that had for us become an American fix. Hamburgers were more than just a food, they were an essential part of the American scene. This was in the years before pizza took its stranglehold on American fast food consumption.

Our own Hamburger Heaven was Kewpees, where we went first with our parents, most likely alone with our mothers, shopping for clothes or school supplies, followed next by the White Tower, the perfect hamburger joint for us. Not long after came the excitement of occasionally driving with a car full of friends to the A & W stand on the South Side. By then pool playing had also entered our lives. The Star Restaurant on State Street, between Superior and La Salle, was the first such destination, with its pool parlor at the rear of the restaurant. It was there we first encountered State Street Harry, the pool shark, who sometimes gave us tips between his money games, consenting to play us for the price of the rack—10 cents—that always came out of one of our pockets,—and happily, because it came with the privilege of watching him at close range. State Street Harry smoked cigars, which, combined with his pool playing skills and smart dress, made him one of the legendary characters of our neighborhood, that included United States Tony and also Bill Miller, who fixed our radios, coming into our homes, dressed in a well-worn suit, with his companionable cigar, that he smoked with elegant ease and expertise.

In our late teens we went for our hamburger fixes to the tiny restaurant, just below street level, at the rear of the Thomas Hotel. Sitting in one of the booths we'd look out at the busy traffic on Marquette Avenue—Howie Sell, Mikey Kaiserlian, Dickie Steberl and myself, seeing ourselves as Hollywood cronies of the silver screen, holding forth with our deluxe, not just every day hamburgers, because these were our evenings together on the town, harboring our newly minted dreams, away from our families, beneath the hotel's blinking neon lights.

The circle completed, the boundaries of the neighborhood navigated, its impact on our lives, or at least my own, revealed, I return to my memory home on Superior Street, to sum up the lasting influences of our neighborhood within the larger neighborhood of our hometown world, to remember first Bill Zaehler and his passion for life, a living magnet, drawing friends, relatives, and even strangers to his busy and cluttered backyard, where I would wander about, visiting his bait shack in back, with minnow tanks, tubs of crabs, and deep buckets of earth worms, also for sale. Whatever it meant to all the others, it was for me a living museum—Uncle Bill's courtyard of magical life unfolding in ordinary time.

Bill's love of music, if not as passionate as his love for the mystery and magic of fishing, was pursued by him with his usual mockery for material gain. Their band, that he was the drummer for, practiced in his home every Wednesday night, the music passing through his wall into ours. For us children, in particular, he was the hero of the block, a legend unto himself, manifesting by style and substance, traits I could not find in any of my own people.

As my personality began to form, I was evaluating myself against all the influences that attracted me, as well as the conditions I felt had stifled me. Like Uncle Bill I was a fisherman, and although I didn't seine for minnows, or catch perch in a net, I did fish for crabs at Island Park with liver purchased from the Boranian grocery store on State Street, around the corner from Garfield School.

Uncle Bill fished by boat, unlike those of us who were limited to fishing with poles. I kept my ready-strung bamboo poles above the rain gutter of our sloping house's roof that faced my mother's arbor. At one word from Uncle Bill that the perch were running, I would make a dash for my poles, jump on my bike and go racing off to the pier.

Uncle Bill had taken a hold on my imagination because he was unlike anyone else I knew, strangely illusive and mysterious, with a devil may care attitude. His goofy, unselfconscious humor, only enhanced his eccentric manner. He could also be moody and aloof. But above all, he was unpredictable and impossible to peg down. Being different had become for me an important virtue, as well as a growing necessity, in my aim to live a life that was truly my own.

My father was an artist of another kind. His art had emerged from both his deep sensitivity, and a sensibility that found order and purpose in the artful preparation and presentation of food. That was the art he had mastered. He was a natural, intuitive cook, who had never studied or read a book on the subject. Perhaps he had learned his trade by osmosis, while a dishwasher at the Thomas Hotel on State Street, from where he was drafted into the service, becoming in time a cook for the Army's brass. I would like to think that it was through the combined influence of my father and Uncle Bill that I became an artist myself, because like them, I was indifferent to material gain, and had my own demons to conquer.

I was seeking to escape the burden of sorrow and defeat that had crushed my people. I did not want to reside in the residue of that tragedy, but to make a real life out of the life I had dreamed for myself, that I was slowly beginning to bring into focus.

My people had come to the right place, beginning anew in America, by refounding the race on the precious soil of freedom. And this was where I belonged. But with this came an obligation. I felt it was up to me to exonerate the losses of my people by developing something in myself that would bring these losses into some kind of balance, by giving our sorrow and suffering the meaning it deserved through an act of transformation and ultimate transcendence. I needed this for all of us, and I needed it for myself. By the age of fifteen I knew that life was a gift, with the realization that this gift was not free but must be paid for.

Thus my life began, with my neighborhood locked inside me, to nourish me and remind me that I was the son of that soil, so alien at the start, until it became in time the permanent ground of my art.

# AFTER AND BEYOND

When I think of the church
and how,
in spite of my indifference,
something of its beauty
had once entered me:
the devout choir of ancient
and inspired voices
stirred something within

before I would dash out the
wide church doors,
(the service concluded)
for the inviting outdoors—
grown magically important
from our confinement within

pausing momentarily for
the wafer on the tongue,
more sublime even than the choir,
transmitting something indelible
from its celestial world—
received in a whisper—

releasing me to be alone
at last, free to wander the wide
world outside all doors.

# Becoming a Writer

# 1.

I had heard that J. I. Case Company came to the docks of New York to hire the Armenians and other émigrés for their factory in Racine, Wisconsin. The story was never corroborated. It had the fictive sound of truth and appealed to my sense of drama.

This is where I began, if there can be said to be beginnings, and if one can extricate one's own history and lore from that of one's father, and then of one's mother, and then at last from all of one's ancestry.

But then my father did not begin his American citizenry as a laborer for J. I. Case, he began as a chef—but even that is not quite right, for it was after serving in the U.S. Army (where he learned to cook) that he became a chef. Upon his discharge he was made an American citizen, and soon after he became a short order cook at Nelson's Hotel. It was only then that he began searching for a mail order bride. Being the sole support of his family—who had fled Turkey for Armenia (where the Massacres stopped but the starvation continued)—and having two wastrel brothers, who were also his dependents, he decided on an orphan bride—one who would not bring further family problems and obligations.

My mother had been the sole survivor of her immediate family, all of them having died of cholera or heartbreak on their forced march from Turkey to the desert wastes of Mesopotamia. My father's family found her in Greece (they were in Piraeus on their way to Armenia) and after a series of refusals which consumed a year, she finally agreed to an engagement by proxy, and thereby said Yes to America (for this is how it must have seemed to her) and No to England, to where she might have gone, having been offered an opportunity for free schooling (college, she said—a dream she would take to her grave, along with some farfetched aristocratic needs, that she thought were her birthright but really belonged to a need in her to balance the loss caused by the horrors of her early life).

Seven years later I was born.

I do not have my own first memory of being—or rather, thinking of myself as an Armenian. Instead, I have a series of memories connected to the dawning realization that I was an American—the realization, that is, that I was American-born, and that the soil I was standing on was therefore America, not Armenia, as I had mistakenly thought. When I was four my mother enrolled me in nursery school at Central Association, to correct the most conspicuous aspect of the problem: I needed to learn English.

By five I was bilingual, but of course I hadn't noticed, as I also had not noticed that a huge psychological problem was beginning to be formed in me.

I do remember an evening when a group of us boys, aged six to eight—the Superior Street gang in embryo: Mikey Kaiserlian, Dickie Steberl, Junior Rognerud, and probably one or more of the Mieneckes—were gathered under the streetlight at the end of our block. All at once God was mentioned, and then at once his nationality was named. Someone insisted that God did not have a nationality, while another claimed that God was American. All at once I knew—or thought I knew—God was Armenian. If I was the son of God, and surely I was, then God was Armenian. Everyone insisted that I was mistaken; the consensus being that either God did not have a nationality, or if He did, He was American.

I felt cheated, deprived, insulted. And that is all I remember, except that the ramifications of that experience would haunt my life—and perhaps I became a writer that night, in order to redress the error that turned into a "fault" in me—for something had been set in my being that night, and it would take years of self-study—for which writing was the means—before I could see and begin to correct this problem, begun so innocently, but that had gone on by momentum and had caused me to spoil everything in my life.

# 2.

It was said that I was a loner. Can this be traced, can anything that belongs to our nature be traced? Or can it only be identified and named and then worked with, if we are to be delivered to a place from which real action and choice can take place?

I remember now my solitary wanderings. I discovered Lake Michigan first, where I fished for perch with all the others, but more importantly I discovered Root River, both from the city bridges, where it often seemed choked and bloated and largely lifeless, until I began traveling outward towards its source, where it was alive with fish and the life that is nurtured by the freedom of moving water. My greatest memories of childhood are memories of fishing. I named two of my books *I Remember Root River* and *Root River Run*. Re-return and then deliverance: the process of inner freedom that cannot be understood unless experienced.

In our homes, in our community, in my immediate and extended surroundings, there was no art, no writing, and no culture but the wisdom of an ancient race living an alien and distorted life. What beauty there was I had to find for myself. Its need was in me and I had therefore to transform the ordinary into something that, although it did not seem to be there, was there, if one could expand one's awareness and see beneath the surface. The invisible world clothed in visible life.

I found it in nature and in the common and preposterous acts of man: my father marching in a parade, the rock-garden across the bridge from Island Park that contained a replica of the bridge I viewed it from, the Saturday matinées at the Main street Theatre, in particular the serials: *Lone Ranger, Batman, Green Hornet, Mark of Zorro,* and many others. But the most special event of all from that time—for it indicated a possibility—was the colored-pencil drawing of an Indian that was done by one of my mother's students during the Armenian language class in the basement of our church. The drawing must have been a gift for my mother, who brought it home to me, never guessing the effect it would have on my life. By now I too was drawing, and it was assumed I would become an artist. I was awarded a blue ribbon for my rendering of a red-headed woodpecker, that resulted in an invitation to study at the Wustum Museum at the edge of town. My only memory of the one or two sessions I attended was that of discomfort, for I had been discriminated against at Garfield Elementary School and by now I hated classrooms of any kind. Had I stayed I would no doubt have studied with Nancy Ekholm Burkert, who, I found out many years later, had also taken classes there with Sylvester Jerry.

# 3.

School. Or to be specific, Garfield Elementary School. I hated it with an unrelenting passion, and for good reason—I was made to feel stupid. Having flunked the second grade, I flunked the fifth grade twice, once in the regular year and then again in summer school. To this day I cannot pass a test, do not know how to listen, and resort to imitation in most things, on the theory that I-will-not-be-able-to-get-it-on-my-own. But then there were sports, and here I excelled. Largely because, like my teammates, I was older (by the time we reached sixth grade all of my Armenian teammates had flunked at least two grades). Ours was the first softball team to win the championship three years running, which meant that we could keep the traveling trophy. And it was our sixth-grade basketball team that scored 100 points in a single game. It had never been done before and probably hasn't been done since. We made the papers and won the championship: Horse Kamakian, Lotch Oglanian, Ed Chobanian, Ralph Molbeck, and myself. All Armenians but one. Our softball coach was Gustave (Shypoke) Sheibach, the janitor, and our basketball coach was Herbert Von Haden, the principal. They respected us and looked out for us and I cherish their memory to this day, as I cherish the memory of my companions.

And then in the sixth grade, finally, there was a teacher who also cared for us—Mrs. McKinney. She read us Mark Twain, and she loved her work—and her work was us. She alone prepared me for Washington Junior High School, there I found myself, quite unexpectedly, at the top of the class. I set a record for the greatest number of book reports given by a seventh grader. The writer I remember best was James Willard Schultz, who wrote countless books about his life as a squaw man.

But then I got bored. The teachers were still horrible, and the routine of being a good student was as deadly as the routine of being an incorrigible one. The fact is I was neither of these things, but what I was I did not know. It was in the ninth grade that we wrote reports on the professions we intended to follow. This was the first and last writing I can remember doing in school. I wrote that I wanted to be a conservationist. I was by now an expert fisherman, and I wanted to be a hunter as well. I flunked typing (my only failure) and went on to Horlick High School. You might say that my preparation for life was proceeding on a decline.

It was on one side or another of my nineteenth birthday, and before the first semester of my junior year of high school was completed, that I walked out of what was for me Incarcerated Hell. I didn't even clean out my locker, and I refused to return to complete my act of departure—despite an admonishing phone call from the principal. It does me no credit to say that I didn't even realize that he was angry. I paid the price of my insensitivity when he refused (a few years later) to honor my Army certificate of high school equivalency, causing me to drive to the South Side of town, where it was honored by our rival, Park High School.

# 4.

I am now nineteen years old, certified stupid, totally unprepared for life, full of great undefined hopes and daydreams, with an unabiding hatred of authority, and hopelessly armed with an upper lip that curls at one corner into a snarl to announce and declare my defiance of the world.

Thus armed I am about to embark—rather clumsily and very luckily—on one of the best years of my life. But not before I am fired from my first attempts at employment. I do not realize, perhaps fortunately, that this will establish a pattern for my life that will endure until I am able to find my own work. But now, after several found and lost jobs, I answered an ad promising travel and adventure, and found myself several stories up in the old Baker Block on Main Street, entering a door marked Crowell-Collier Publishing Company.

I was about to become a door-to-door magazine salesman, traveling throughout Wisconsin and northern Illinois. This was a job I would not have to worry about being fired from: if you produced you ate, and if you didn't, you starved. It was self-producing, self-regulating work. I could not have known then that it was preparing me for an even harder ordeal to come—for the first thing a writer must discipline is himself.

I found myself among a mixed company

of misfits of every cloth and description, Wayne Kruse—who would be my sidekick—had signed on the same week, and together we grafted ourselves to such seasoned veterans as Bob Hill, the cocky ace of the crew, Pliney Olson, the maroon-shirted hobo with aristocratic manners, Charley Metcalf, the pint-sized alcoholic for whom the manager—Milton (Smitty) Smith—had a soft spot, and also Max Dembroski, who was our field manager. This was the nucleus, around which others came and went: newcomers who lasted only a week or a month, as well as veteran travelers, who followed the sun and their own lazy natures.

My first week on the job I sold twenty orders and joined the magic circle (from which I would soon plummet), making the mimeo newsletter that traveled the circuit. An order was worth $5 to the salesman, and $100 in 1951 was Big Money. It wouldn't happen often, but it didn't need to, for the great excitement was not money but adventure. And romance. I fell in love with the life, beginning with my first drink in a tavern—the famous Mully's American Bar, which was downstairs and next door to the Baker Building. And then I fell in love with all of the cities, concluding with Janesville, Smitty's home (he lived with his family in the old Park Hotel that was run by his wife), which became my favorite city of all, for it was there I fell in love with Smitty's daughter, Barbara.

About this time Max Dembroski left, not being cut out for the game, and I was named field manager, "The youngest in the history of Crowell-Collier Publishing Company," the mimeo said. I bought my first car, a gray 1941 Plymouth with a sailboat hood ornament. How I scraped together $200 for the purchase I cannot imagine, unless the company chipped in half. My job consisted of driving the crew from city to city, registering at the local police station, where we were fingerprinted, checking the crew into a hotel (the weekly rates at the best hotels in town was twenty dollars average—and we always went first class, doubling up when we had a bad week, but taking our own room when we didn't), placing the men in their territories, verifying orders, drying out the drunks, making reports, and paying the men on Saturday mornings when the vouchers from the home office reached the territory.

It lasted an entire year, until I got drafted into the Army. I would never again experience such camaraderie and adventure and high-spirited innocent fun. I felt worldly, cocky, and ready for anything.

Anything but the Army, that is. Here my innocence was shattered. There was something deadlier and dirtier than school, after all. But then wasn't the Army as well a part of society's education? Hadn't we merely traded in the spinster teacher, full of prejudice and hatred, for the bully-boy sergeant, but with the stakes and the risks suddenly and dangerously escalated?

Once again I was forced to rebel.

And once again something saved me—for, as the Armenian proverb goes, God never closes every door. In my final week as a magazine salesman I discovered Theodore Dreiser. The book was *The Stoic.* I was beside myself with an excitement that bordered on shock. It was as if everything I had been groping for and secretly believing/hoping existed, not only did exist, was not only true and possible, but had been made manifest by a man in a book. It had to do with Being—that I knew. And that was all I knew. The written word, the book, became for me a god. Something did exist that had the power to deliver me to another reality, for a truth that was somehow already within me, but buried, unrealized, and without a means for expression and ultimate usage.

Had it not been for that book at that particular moment it is hard to say what would have become of me. I was far less prepared for the Army than I had been for school—although I was as innocent as a babe entering kindergarten.

We gathered at Memorial Hall in Racine and were driven by bus to Fort Sheridan. The first days were tolerable, partially because I shared a barracks with old friends: Sam Balian, Jerry Hansen, Johnny Musurlian, and Jack Levonian, among others. Then we were shipped to Fort Knox, where from the start, I began to show my stripes—no pun intended. I skipped reveille whenever I could, and in the middle of maneuvers I would wander off by myself. I refused to listen, I refused to learn. I was on the golf course when news reached me that I was being shipped to Korea.

I remember my mother and father standing

on the porch, waving good-bye, as a neighbor drove me to the airport to catch my plane for Seattle. They were sure I would never return and they were powerless to do anything about it (this was Korea, remember, not Vietnam). Father had told Mother, "He'll fall asleep on guard duty, they'll shoot him." He was right about the first part, but he didn't know his son. Once, while guarding officers' quarters, I sneaked into the colonel's room and fell asleep on the chair beside his bed. If he woke up, I figured I would wake up, too. I'd say I heard something under his bed.

The ship bound for Korea took thirteen days to make its first port—Japan. I was AWOL the entire time. I cannot remember now what precipitated my decision. Was there duty I wanted to get out of; did I want to eat wherever and whenever I could; was the puking in the cramped quarters getting to me; or was it simply that I wanted to sit on deck and watch the ocean, which I was seeing for the first time?

It wasn't long before I was missed, and a search was put into effect. Passes were issued for meals, bulletins went out and calls were made over the loudspeaker. Everyone was being questioned. A few of the soldiers knew who I was but they, more than all the others, were enjoying the game, and they were not about to turn me in. I found a different place to sleep every night, and different places to eat as well.

It got to be amusing. On the last night I thought I would enjoy the pleasure of my own arrest, so I got in a line that was being checked by the lieutenant in charge of my case. I couldn't suppress a smile when I stood in front of him and told him my name.

He sputtered, "Put this man under arrest." There weren't any MP's in sight, and so the job fell to an innocent private, who fumbled my arm and tried to look stern and in possession of himself. I was marched to the kitchen where the mess sergeant was ordered to make me work through the night at KP.

The mess sergeant was huge, black, and inscrutable. I stood before him and waited. He turned and walked away without speaking until the others had left the kitchen. Then he said, "Whats you wants to eat, boy?"

I sat down before a dish of fresh-baked apple pie, enjoying the taste of fame. The climax was yet a week away, but the following day, while walking to the PX, I passed the lieutenant who had arrested me. He was so flustered when he saw me he saluted. I didn't return his salute, instead I smiled faintly and walked on, without breaking my stride. I thought, "What can they do, send me to Korea!"

One week later all of the five thousand pathetic souls that had journeyed over the waters—that I alone had enjoyed—were given their orders: Korea—except for five hundred men, of which I (of all people) was numbered. We would remain in Japan. My life had been saved, for looking back on it now I know that I would never have returned from Korea alive.

# 5.

The Korean Conflict, as it was called, had ended; my two years were up, and I was discharged. I returned home, thoroughly disillusioned with life, my nerves shot, and with no prospects or plans for the future. Reading had kept me alive in the Army, and now, aged twenty-three, I began a novel of my own. My subject was the Kaiserlians—the troubled, eccentric, colorful family that had had such a strong influence on my youth. I had this idea that I could solve their problems by writing a novel about their life. It was a preposterous idea and it fizzled to a halt by page twenty-five. I now knew for myself the great gulf that lay between writing home and writing fiction. I had discovered in the Army that I enjoyed writing letters, and also that I was good at it. I don't remember now all the people I wrote to, but it remains vivid in my memory that Joyce Southwell (who must have taken it on as a morale-building assignment) was the one I counted on receiving letters from, and the person I most enjoyed writing to. There was nothing at stake, nothing to be gained or lost, and so I simply wrote, letter after letter, indulging my newly discovered bent for writing.

But a novel! It would be several years before I would try to write anything creative again.

There was something to be learned—but

just what it was and how it was to be acquired remained a mystery.

I went back to being nervous. My mother's cooking was too rich for me, our house too cramped, and once again I found myself being fired from one job after another.

What to do?

I knew that I could get $110.00 a month if I attended college. I had already gotten my high school equivalency exam certified, and I learned that the University of Wisconsin had a two-year extension course downtown.

The GI Bill, as I believe it was called, combined with what I was making selling shoes Friday evenings and Saturdays at Mary Jane's Shoe Store, would be enough for my purposes.

Everyone said you had to have a college degree if you wanted to get ahead. If "ahead" was the place to get to, then I wanted to get there, too. I wanted to show "them," whoever "they" were, that I could "do it." I had forgotten, temporarily, about being a writer. But in the second semester I took a composition class and it became clear to everyone that I could write.

Time moves slowly when you are not sure what you want, or even how to get what you think you do want. It was a sad and boring year, drinking every night, going to class hung-over, contemplating suicide, hating Racine and my life—and the prospect of doing the same thing all over again the following year seemed senseless. Where I got the idea I do not know, but I decided to go to Europe.

I drove to Bridgeport, Connecticut, to visit an old Army buddy, got a night time job at Sikorsky Aircraft (building helicopter propellers) and worked as a busboy in their cafeteria afternoons. Before leaving home I had cashed out an insurance policy my mother had on me (worth $500.00) and after six months of hard work I had $1,500 to my name—a lot of money! I booked passage on the Queen Elizabeth and went to Europe for four months, traveling first to England and then to nearly every country on the continent. It was the-wildest-of-dreams-come-true! Europe at that time (1954) was everything America was not: cultured, sophisticated, with great restaurants to eat in, wine to drink and learn about, sights to see, and best of all friendships and adventure. And of course romance. I bought a notebook and wrote in it every night.

I need to back up for a moment and remember my six months in Connecticut, because it was during this time that I discovered New York, and the experience (one in particular) that prepared me for Europe. I visited New York often on weekends in order to go to jazz clubs, theaters, art galleries and museums—and it was at the Metropolitan that I saw my first work of original art. I had mounted the stairs, and walking down the corridor I saw ahead of me in one of the rooms, a painting by Van Gogh. I knew about art through reproductions but I had no idea! I literally stopped in my tracks, so overcome with emotion that I could not move. It was an experience on the level of my first reading of Theodore Dreiser. Again a flower unknown to me peeled back another petal and revealed a portion of its heart that was my own heart. Although I had not forgotten that I wanted to write, I suddenly found myself plunged into the world of art, and once I reached Europe I began visiting museum after museum, feeding a hunger so deeply buried that it had as yet no name or identity.

I had hoped to find work in Europe but it was not to be, so I returned again to boring and hopeless America. I re-enrolled in college, my reasons for doing so unchanged—there was simply nothing better to do. But there were two subjects now that interested me: writing and art history. I went from selling shoes to tending bar. And I continued to read on my own. College itself meant nothing to me but a paycheck, although I did have an idea in the back of my head that a degree was important, perhaps even necessary, to have. Had I been able to trust my own experience and intelligence I would have seen the utter absurdity and futility of college life and college learning.

I don't think any writer worth his salt ever learned to write in college, and whether or not I believed, or even thought about this at the time, I will say this: it never occurred to me even to try.

I scribbled on in secret, and for my third year of schooling I went to Madison, where I enjoyed for the second time in my life a camaraderie with friends of like spirit (Ardie Kaiserlian, Ted Burdosh, Jerry Zwiefel and Jack Danelski). It would last for only one year. During the following summer my father was stricken with cancer and so I transferred to the University of Wisconsin in Milwaukee in order to be near the Veteran's Hospital.

My father was to live another year, and then, before the start of my final term, my mother and sister moved to Fresno. By now my Uncle Jack, who had been a second father to me, had also died. There was talk of my inheriting his 1924 Model-A Ford (that he had bought new), as his son Chuckie had years before inherited my Red Racer bicycle. But upon his death it somehow got itself interred in the garage beyond the garden he had loved so much.

Had I noticed—had I been able to notice—I would have seen that the old world was coming to an end. But I hadn't yet made the beginning of a new world for myself.

On the day following my final exam I got in my car and drove to California. I knew what I needed to do next: meet William Saroyan. I had discovered his books, and through them had rediscovered my heritage. Now I needed to meet him, although I did not as yet know the reasons why.

# 6.

A writer's apprenticeship is a never-ending thing. It cannot be chosen—as apprenticeship—because it is impossible to know what it is, or how to acquire it, or how it ends and when it will end—or even if it ever will end: that is, when/if it will turn into writing, and then evolve into writing that will sell (it is assumed it will fulfill its other purpose, if there is another purpose—and there must be another purpose for the great fight to have been worth the waging), or even what the final form of that writing will be.

I had read and read and read. I had traveled and would continue to travel, I had listened everywhere to the speech patterns of people, and I had practiced dialogue. But above all I had tried to understand how the artist could transform life into literature; that is, chaos into order, the stuff of ordinary existence into the imperishable materiality of extraordinary art.

Saroyan was about to leave for Europe when I arrived in San Francisco, but I was not deterred. I had begun his bibliography and I wrote to tell him so. By now I was collecting his books. I had to own them all and read them all. And then I moved to Fresno to manage The Book House on Tulare Street where I could meet and know the people and places that were the subjects and objects of Saroyan's art. I wanted to see, if I could, how his writing was done, for up until now all I had managed on my own that I considered "creative" were two finished stories and what I suppose would have to be called a poem.

More than twenty years later, upon Saroyan's death and at the bidding of my hometown newspaper, I would write:

> ... I had arrived on the scene just in
> time, because the old Armenian
> town was still standing, with the
> churches and bakeries and dairies
> and assorted buildings that he had
> written about, still somehow intact.
>
> And not only were the streets still there,
> carrying their immortal
> names, but the courthouse was still
> standing with the postal telegraph
> office facing it, just as I had found it in
> *The Human Comedy*.
>
> It was all there and I went out to all of it, to
> unravel, if I could,
> the mystery of writing.

Saroyan came and went. We met and talked and I kept pecking away at his bibliography. It was finished at last and published in 1965. I had returned once again to San Francisco, and now, with my book circulating in the great world, I received a letter one day from an editor in New York proposing a bibliography of some of the Beat poets living in San Francisco.

But I seem to have gotten ahead of myself, for the memory of that offer by an editor I had never met reminds me of one of the handful of important decisions I have made in my life. It had occurred a few years earlier at an employment agency in Chicago. Having failed to find meaningful work in San Francisco, not yet having begun to write, and suddenly feeling homesick and lost, I packed my car and began the long drive home. Everyone said I should be able to get a good job on the strength of my degree, especially in a big city like Chicago. But the questions I was being asked by the man in the agency were disturbing me. At one point he asked me to turn around and look at something in the corner of the room. Then he asked to see my hand. He was examining my fingernails apparently, and when I had turned he had looked to see if my neck was cleanly shaved.

I felt degraded by the interview, and by the time I reached the street I had made an irrevocable decision: I would never again in my life fill out an application form. Instead, I would work at my life until my name itself became what I was and what I would be employed for. It was a bold, desperate decision. It meant, as I knew, that I would never seek regular employment again, that I would have to drift from job to job.

I couldn't have known at the time that this decision would give my apprenticeship the boost it needed. It was now do-or-die, which is the perfect framework and condition for a near-impossible goal. No one in my line had been a writer, no one I knew had been a writer. Racine had never produced a writer, I myself had not yet even met a writer—and writing I was convinced, was the highest activity of man.

Who did I think I was to imagine I could become a writer? The few people I mentioned it to looked at me with either scorn or pity. I decided that in the future I would keep it to myself.

I remained in Racine for one year, opened a used bookstore called The Sign of the Tiger, sold shoes at Zahn's, and tended bar at the Hotel Racine—where I met my first writer, Glenway Wescott. But the most important thing about that year was that I began to look at my city with a writer's eye.

Everywhere I looked there was a story, and everywhere I looked I saw the remnants of my own confused past. How could meaning and order and beauty be brought to bear on this life—and this city—that I both loved and hated? And what was its truth? And who was I? And how could I use writing to help me in my search?

I struggled. I drifted. I dreamed. I waited. And I watched.

Ted Burdosh, my college chum, whose home was in northern Wisconsin, had talked to me about trout fishing. Ted was an expert fly caster and when he invited me to his parents' home in Little Suamico for a weekend of trout fishing, I readily accepted. I did not think then that at the age of thirty a completely new, totally unknown experience would still be possible for me.

I stood on a high bank and looked down at my first trout stream: swift, crystal clear, pure and undefiled. It was the single most beautiful sight I had witnessed in nature, in great part because it was the home of fish, and not just any fish, but the swift and speckled leaping trout.

One other memory of that year, very different from the above, stands out as an influence that would also effect my life. Ardie Kaiserlian and I were watching a boxing match on television. It might have been Jake La Motta's last fight, and he was taking a merciless beating. He had somehow stayed on his feet (he had managed an entire career without once being knocked down) for the entire fight. When it was finally over he was asked at ringside why he hadn't gone down for a nine-count in order to take a rest. As I recall he replied, "I didn't want to start any bad habits."

I had just been given my first piece of literary advice. My worst beatings were yet ahead of me, but I knew to stand my ground, no matter what. What Jake La Motta had said to me was, Don't set a bad precedent for yourself, establish good working habits and don't let yourself off.

# 7.

Back to San Francisco, 1965. Who were the Beat poets? And what was poetry for that matter? I had taken more English courses than philosophy (my major) and so, inevitably, I had read some poets. I did like Yeats, along with Housman, and—I am embarrassed to say—Khalil Gibran and Walter Benton. But none of this had prepared me for contemporary American poetry.

In my last year of college I had heard of Allen Ginsberg and Jack Kerouac, but neither of them were in San Francisco when I got there, and although Allen Ginsberg soon showed up. Gregory Corso also left town, but there were plenty of others to choose from.

The poets I finally settled on for my book were David Meltzer (who was the only one I knew personally—he was working at Discovery Book Store and I would soon be working there as well), Michael McClure, Gary Snyder, Philip Whalen, Brother Antoninus (William Everson), and Lawrence Ferlinghetti, whose City Lights Bookstore was two doors down from Discovery.

*The* David Meltzer Monograph was published with a frontispiece drawing of the poet by my friend Peter LeBlanc. I had stolen a line ("otter brown eyes") from a short story in typescript by another friend, Jerry (Jacob) Needleman, who was also trying to write. His wife Carla, said I had been hiding my light under a bushel basket. Jerry and I decided to begin a literary magazine. He had the perfect title, *Tired Horse Review*, as I remember. He thought the title so outstanding that he swore me to secrecy, and together we sat down to write our credo. I put a piece of paper in the typewriter and ten minutes later, presto! A perfect manifesto. From that day on Jerry was convinced I was a born writer.

I visited Gary Snyder's class at Berkeley, Brother Antoninus at his monastery in Marin County, Phil Whalen at his apartment on Beaver Street, Michael McClure at Holmes' Bookstore in Oakland, where Bob Hawley (the publisher of Oyez, who brought two of my portraits out in chapbooks) worked, and finally, Lawrence Ferlinghetti at his studio on Portreo Hill. Even if I didn't think much of the Beat poetry generally, it was still a very high time in my life. Jack Spicer was holding court nightly at Gino & Carlo's tavern, where I began to drink and play pool with other unknown writers like myself. Richard Brautigan was writing *Trout Fishing in America.* I had considered including him in my book but disqualified him on the basis of his poems, that seemed to me minimal at best—but we had long, involved talks about Saroyan, whose work he admired as much as I did.

As I went on with the writing of the book I began to see that the thing that interested me most about these poets was not so much their writing but their manhood. It seemed to me that it wasn't enough to be a good writer—or good at anything else—what mattered most was a man's character and Being. I felt that if a man did important work then he himself should be the equal of that work. The outside should match the inside. For good or ill, the writing of the portraits for that book was founded on that premise.

The book was finally completed, and at the same time I sold my Saroyan collection to the Fresno Public Library. I had $5,000 in my pocket and, at the same time, a publishing offer from Kent Sate University Press for *Six Poets of the San Francisco Renaissance.* Once again I packed my car and headed for Racine, where I showed the letter from Kent State to my childhood friend, Chuck Pehlivanian, who was now a lawyer. Kent State wanted to put the word "Beat" in the title, and they had offered me a $500.00—with a tiny royalty, as I remember. I didn't want to make a title change, and I didn't think $500.00 was enough money for a year's work. I asked Chuck to do something about it. Whatever it was he did, the offer was rescinded and I went off to Europe for the summer, wondering if I had done the right thing.

But first I lingered in Racine, visiting old haunts and gathering material from a past that seemed to be increasing its hold on me. I wrote "Highway America" that would eventually become the booklet, *An Evening with Saroyan.*

By the time I boarded a Belgian freighter in Pensacola, Florida, I had visited six southern states. I sold my Volkswagen in New Orleans, but in Germany I bought another and drove slowly, leisurely, to Greece, where I spent a very happy month in the city of Pylos on the sea, and met Erik Haugaard and his family. Erik was working mornings on a novel, but from afternoon till evening he, along with his wife Myrna and their two sprightly children, with me in tow, drove to a secluded beach, where on a particular day we heard sheep's bells approaching over a hillock, to roam over the road ahead of our halted car. Knowingly or not I was living the life of a writer.

# 8.

I had this idea that I would not marry until I had established my life work. I wanted the woman I married to know what she was getting, and I wanted her to understand that she was getting something special. I was by now nearing my middle thirties, but I still knew very little about life. I had always been naive, which my mother was wont to excuse by declaring that I had a "good heart." Alas, it didn't make me less a fool.

As I journeyed home from Europe I sensed that the time of my marriage was approaching. But the marriage I made was doomed from the start. When it finally ended I couldn't help but believe that it never should have happened. While it was on and after it was over, its result for me seemed to be nothing but pain, suffering and remorse. But there is no school for marriage but marriage itself, and it was because of my suffering and remorse that I was able to marry Nonny Hogrogian, a woman my age, who was also an artist, and whose ancestry was the same as mine. It was proof of graduation. My "failed" marriage had resulted in my making a true and real marriage.

But it was my first marriage that helped me to become a poet. There is a reason why poetry, love, and youth are connected in our minds. Perhaps one has to be mad to write poetry, and being in love makes this madness seem desirable.

I had not yet become the writer of my writing but now—at once—something that appeared to be writing was occurring to me. I found myself wandering out of the house and into the back yard, and then wandering back inside, where I would scribble something on paper that seemed to have something to do with what I had just seen. It was all very confusing. I didn't know what poetry was, but whatever it was I couldn't imagine that I was writing it. And yet there was nothing else to call the stuff I was getting down on paper—and in fact, in its form at least, it did look like poetry.

Saroyan and I had made a friendship, which began about the time I started writing *Six Poets of the San Francisco Renaissance*, for which he would contribute an introduction. He had admired the writing—in part, I am sure, because it was so unlike the kind of writing he did. He had been away while I was writing my poems, but upon his return he phoned and ask that I come over to his place—he was the owner of two adjoining tract houses in Fresno, one for his papers and junk, the other for his living. Fortunately, before leaving, I thought to take a sheaf of poems with me. Surely, the Master would know what I had done and whether or not my poems were any good. He had let me know on an earlier occasion that my short stories, although showing talent, were not publishable.

Saroyan, as it turned out, had called to offer me a job as his secretary, but immediately after reading my poems he changed his mind. I had my own writing to do now, he said (he had called the poems "A-1"), and my writing, combined with my plans for my press, would be full time work. I had founded The Giligia Press (named after my father's birthplace, which was the site of the last Armenian kingdom) in order to make money from my book (it did), and now Saroyan was able to see something I myself had not yet seen: I would soon be publishing poetry—my own—and, inevitably, the work of other poets with whom I would feel a kinship. This kind of literary practice (for poets, especially) seemed to be in the American tradition, as I was soon to learn.

Poem followed poem, while the proceeds from my book kept us afloat. One day Andy Brown, whom I had met at Discovery Book Store, and who had helped me get a job as literary consultant at Northwestern University (the twenty-five dollar a week unemployment checks resulting from this job had given me the money with which to write my book about the poets) called to say he had purchased Gotham Book Mart and asked if I would come and help him out.

My wife and I set out at once by car, stopping on the way to visit her relatives in New Mexico. To make a long story short, I fell in love with New Mexico, and after our brief stay in New York we moved to Santa Fe, for what would prove to be a very important year in my life. I had done very little writing in New York (the place didn't agree with me) but now I was writing again—poems about the haunting landscape of New Mexico, so different and stranger than anything I had previously seen or experienced.

Santa Fe was a city with a culture, a past, and a tradition. I began meeting other writers with whom I exchanged views and shared my work. Then I met Gerald Hausman, an unpublished poet like myself, and a student in Las Vegas, New Mexico. It wasn't long before we gave our first poetry reading—at a coffee shop off campus, that we followed with a reading at St. John's College in Santa Fe, celebrating the event with a chapbook of poems.

There is an inestimable value in the friendships beginning writers make. They share their hopes and dreams, and knowing each other's work intimately, they are able to keep each other honest, while boosting morale and providing an audience for one another. This kind of sharing and healthy criticism can happen but once in a writer's life—for once you are published you are alone and compelled to know for yourself what you are doing, as well as when you go off and how to get back on.

But the real fun is in the beginning days, because, so much of it being dreams, anything seems possible and perhaps everything is possible. Gerry Hausman's enthusiasm for poetry in general and my own in particular, was the greatest benefit I could have received at what was certainly a crucial time in my life. I had a friend in the literary wars, a comrade-in-arms.

I had been living in Santa Fe for one year when I learned there was an Armenian oud player living in Albuquerque, who had in turn learned there was an Armenian poet living in Santa Fe.

The oud player turned out to be Avak Akgulian, the great oral historian of the folkways of the people of Racine, in particular the Armenians. We soon got together and as he talked his stories began evoking in me a longing for something—I knew not what. I was not where I needed to be. There was something calling me. I realized that it had to do with my people, it had to do with my childhood, and it had to do with an understanding of my past—without which I could not inhabit the future.

I had by now written the poem, "On the Death of My Father," and soon after my meeting with Avak I had a dream about my father that I tried to get into a poem. In the dream he is standing in front of me . . . "his back to me bare." What did it mean? After a great deal of pondering I realized that I needed to see the Armenians again.

We packed and moved once again to Fresno.

# 9.

During my years as an antiquarian book dealer I had gotten to know Henry Madden, the head librarian at Fresno State College. I went to him now and asked for a part-time job as a library consultant. It was a time when libraries had been allocated more money than they knew how to reasonably spend.

The pay was poor but the hours were right and I set to work writing the poems I felt I had been called to write. Every evening, immediately after dinner, I would go to my work room and write for a minimum of three hours.

After four months' time *Homage to Adana* was completed. In writing this book I had found my material and my voice. I also learned how to take a theme and sustain it for the length of an entire book. From here on, this would characterize all of my books of poetry—they would not be collections of poems—a book being the excuse to gather them together—but a book in the way that a novel or a biography is a book.

Still another thing happened while writing that book: my mind finally came forward and took its proper place alongside my feelings. It felt as if my mind had finally caught up, and as it did, I realized why it had taken me so long to become a writer—I had been mentally unprepared. Or should I say, developed.

We are a body, we are a mind, and we are also our feelings. When all three participate in an activity it has a quality and force that no one part—no matter how highly developed it may be—can bring. But now with my mind and my feelings suddenly aligned, I wondered, what was the function of the mysterious third ingredient, the body. It took a long time before I found the answer, but at last I saw what it was—the breath. It made me wonder if our only mark of individuality is not our breath. We are breathed into life, and we are all breathed differently. In poetry, all talk of cadence, music, measure, line break etc., is really talk of breath. We write as we breath, for as we breathe we write. This is how the body accompanies the mind and feelings, as they participate together in the act of making a poem.

There was another reason why it had taken me so long to come to my writing, which *Homage to Adana* also made evident, revealing once and for all what the subject of my writing would be: myself. This of course had been the reason for my attraction to Saroyan's work. I had a deep, abiding need to understand my life—and writing, I instinctively knew, was the instrument through which I would conduct my search. But this by itself was not enough: writing had to be interesting to others as well, and this being the case how, I wondered if my writing would ever qualify in the marketplace, since here I was a son of immigrant parents, and a person who not only did not have any special qualities of his own, but one who had in fact gotten himself raised in what amounted to a ghetto, in a city that had to be one of the most forlorn places in all America.

These attitudes—call them beliefs—were in my bones. My mother remembered my accosting her when I was ten tears old, with the accusation that there were no great men in Racine. She said our great men had been assassinated by the Turks. What about the Americans then, I had asked, what was their excuse? I needed models, figureheads, examples—and there were none in sight.

All of these notions, I knew, had kept me from writing. But little by little, principally through a gradual understanding of Saroyan's work, I began to see that for the purpose of art one life is as good as another, and that no life is unworthy of the attention of art.

I had my models all along, as the writing of *Homage to Adana* would reveal. I had them because I had to have them, and so I had, unwittingly, transformed the material that surrounded me as a child into something meaningful, instructive, and intelligent for myself. The river, the lake, the rock gardens, the pavilions and gazebos—all of nature itself—as well as the people I knew: United States Tony, Umbashi, Joe Perch, State Street Harry—there was a meaning to their lives. There was a meaning to their lives for me. It was so because I required it, and because I did, they would become what they needed to be for me.

I had learned to make a poem, and because I had, I was beginning to find out about my life. It seemed obvious to me now that a man could live a lifetime and never get the first twelve years of his life understood. And yet, those years would determine everything that followed. Nearly all of my writing from now on would be concerned with an attempt to do just that.

Soon after I completed *Homage to Adana*, James Baloian, a young poet who had studied with Philip Levine and Robert Mezey at Fresno State College, approached me with the suggestion that we do a poetry magazine together. I was against doing a magazine, but I had another idea: Because of the times, and because of all the teacher-poets—we could make, an interesting city anthology.

It was a new concept in publishing. By now The Giligia Press was going strong. I had published several books of poetry—so why, I reasoned, not do an anthology to add to the list. Together, Baloian and I selected work from the twenty best local poets we could find. Then we got Tom Peck to bring his camera down to the old Santa Fe train station to photograph the poets in the book, to which we added the presences of William Saroyan and William Everson as elder statesman-poets who hailed from the Valley.

It was a happy moment, and no one, least of all myself, suspected that we were making history. A hundred and more city anthologies followed from all over the country, as poets everywhere saw that they didn't have to be dependent on traditional publishing procedures to get their work out into the world. We titled our book, *Down at the Santa Fe*

*Depot: 20 Fresno Poets.* It was an instant success locally, selling out the first thousand copies in one month. By good timing or fortune it was issued almost simultaneously with my first book of poems, to which Saroyan added an introduction, after he changed the title from *A Family of Four* to *On the Death of My Father and Other Poems.* I had arrived: I was a poet, a publisher, and I had made a name in the world—just as I had vowed I would.

# 10.

The year was 1970. My life was changing, and changing fast. The dissolution of my marriage had finally occurred. I read Castaneda's *Don Juan: A Yaqui Way of Knowledge*, which would influence my next book of poems, but more important, would show me, both through the teachings of that book and the indications revealed by my own poems, that there was another level of life that was beckoning me.

I had moved to Lenox, Massachusetts, and I took up residence with the Hausmans at Windsor Mountain School, where Gerry was teaching—its campus being the summer home of the resident musicians at Tanglewood, just down the road. There I wrote *Looking Over Hills* in a month's time, and realized that the "higher states" in which poets often find themselves when creating, do not belong to them, cannot be beckoned at will, and in fact, the poet at such times is nothing more than a radio transmitting messages between levels of reality. I knew—that is to say, I was convinced—from having read Castaneda, that these states could only be achieved by being earned. A poet was a channel, yes, but nothing was his for the keeping. A need was growing in me—a need I could not name but that was nonetheless mysteriously knowable. By the end of that summer I was offered the editorship of *Ararat*, the Armenian-American literary magazine. For some years I had been reviewing books and contributing poems to their pages, and I had some very definite ideas about changes that needed to be made in the magazine—both to serve its audience and community, and to fulfill the needs of writers like myself who were grappling with their past. I was beginning to see that my Armenian heritage had been, from the very beginning of my life, both a blessing and a curse.

The first thing I did when I got to the Armenian General Benevolent Union in Manhattan, where *Ararat* was published, was to call Nonny Hogrogian on the phone. She was an outstanding illustrator, famous for her children's books. I was hoping she would agree to do the jacket illustration for *Homage to Adana*.

We knew of each other's work. She was pleased to hear from me, but realizing that it would be a labor of love, she recommended another well-known Armenian-American artist, saying she was on deadline with a new book. While I was dialing the number she gave me, she called back on an open line, and said she would like to see the manuscript. As she tells the story, she fell in love with me through my poetry, and after finishing the illustration, asked me to come for lunch, after she had completed the etching for my book. It amazes me to this day that the first thing I said to her after I sat down, was to ask her birth year. When she replied that she was a Taurus, I said, without thinking. "Oh, it would never work, my ex-wife was a Taurus." I had just found my soul mate, but I was completely oblivious to the state this had put me in. The question I had asked her had come directly from my subconscious without troubling to check in with my ordinary state of consciousness.

Several days passed before we got together again, but within that time I had written my first poem for what would soon become *The Nonny Poems.* This would become the book's first poem:

The First Day

We had lunch with white
wine and cheese. I brought
that. You made the soup.
Armenian olives and bread.
And the mezas you served
in small Oriental bowls.

When it was done, and after
we had talked, I put on my
hat and then removed it at
the door to give you a
parting hug and kiss on
the cheek.

First hours, then days
later I began to realize
that nothing is as casual
as that for which the end
is not yet written.

Nonny was on deadline with her book of Grimm Tales, but we were now a pair, and while she drew I wrote, and the day after she turned her book in we went to City Hall with a friend and got married.

# 11.

From New Hampshire, where we took up residence after our marriage in 1971, we moved to upstate New York. My poems now were concerned exclusively with the present, and they began to unfold as naturally as breathing. Had I really done the impossible, had I resolved my early life and made it possible for me to inhabit the present: with art and with living? The poems, for the moment, seemed to say so. And yet there was the search for something more that had begun with the reading of that strange book by Castaneda composed of fact and fiction, that gave the lie to both, thereby creating a new reality. And it was this reality, I felt, that I had come in touch with when I wrote my Berkshire poems, that were so unlike any of my previous work.

Then one day I began writing poems of my childhood again—but so different from the poems in the previous volume, that had been content only to look back. The first poem I wrote would serve as the book's epigraph:

> At the bottom of Liberty Street,
> the Island Park Bridge—
> (the hollow heart of the city);
> and I return there now for
> the soundings:

pavilion dead, river dead,
city all but dead,
with only the breathless
remains of the imitation
rock-garden city in the yard
almost touching the bridge
it imitates (on which I stand)
and there,
on that spot—
just beyond the heart
but palpitating with it, the
new city, the city that
sings these poems,
is going up

I had returned again, but this time to reclaim my life. I had payed homage to the past, and now, with the poems of *I Remember Root River*, I had slain the demon that would hold me to that past. I was ready to declare my life.

Just a month before I had completed *Taking the Soundings on Third Avenue*, concluding (though I hadn't known it then) the trilogy of poems that began with *The Nonny Poems* and that was followed by *Any Day of Your Life*.

Three was a good number, two was not. But now, without any thought that there would be a fitting and concluding third volume to my childhood poems, my writing life suddenly changed. Ever since I was a little boy my mother had said to me, "Someday you grow up and tell my story." No doubt this lament echoed through all of the surrounding homes in our community. How the other children responded I did not know. I only knew that for me her story was too painful to listen to; it was a hell she had passed through, that I had no intention of entering.

And so here I was, well past the age of forty, never having heard her story of persecution and starvation, but with the promise made at last, that since I was a writer, even though only a poet, to bear witness to her life.

I flew my mother to New York so I could hear about her life for the first time. She arrived clutching her story in hand: Fourteen handwritten pages in Armenian. We began by taping the reading of her script. When she came to the part of her story where her mother dies of a broken heart she began weeping—the first time ever in my presence—and said, "I cannot any more today."

I could see that this was going to be a book of suffering but I did not see then that, because the suffering was ours, the reader would be the beneficiary.

It is the writer I would come to understand, that must suffer, not the reader.

One year later the book was completed and upon its acceptance I phoned my mother to give her the news. But apparently she and her family already knew, as her dream of the night before had made known. She said, "Last night in my dream my entire family was gathered into a circle and Virginia (my kid sister) was moving inside our circle and pouring tea into each of our cups. This is the first dream I have ever had where all of my family was present. As Virginia poured tea into each of our cups I could see a look of peace come over all of their faces. David, it is because of your book. Now there is rest and joy and peace for our family at last."

*The Road From Home* would go on to make my name, but long before it won any awards—in fact while it was still in typescript—my mother declared, "Now you can go on and write anything." And suddenly I saw that it was true. I would not only be able to write both poetry and fiction but in any other genre I might choose. I had found a way at last to make a living exclusively from writing. I had never questioned the inability of poetry to do this for me, because I never had a choice: I had not chosen poetry, it had chosen me, providing me with the means and direction I needed to pursue my aim. But as my life began expanding so did my skills. The pursuit and the purpose of my life remained —to know myself, to be myself, and to fulfill my destiny here on Earth as the son of God—that I knew first as a child that I was.

## ABOUT THE AUTHOR

David Kherdian is the author and editor of over seventy books, that include poetry, novels, memoirs, biographies, retellings, and children's books. His anthologies include *Beat Voices*, and three seminal works: *Down at the Santa Fe Depot: 20 Fresno Poets*, that inspired a series of regional anthologies, *Settling America: The Ethnic Expression of 14 Contemporary Poets*, and *Forgotten Bread: Armenian American Writers of the First Generation.* With his wife, two-time Caldecott Medalist, Nonny Hogrogian, they were the publishers of three small presses, and as editor / art director, three disparate journals: *Ararat: A Quarterly*, *Forkroads: A Journal of Ethnic-American Literature*, and *Stopinder: A Gurdjieff Journal for Our Time*. He has, with his presses, journal and anthologies, along with his own work, helped place ethnic writing into the canon of American literature.

His many awards include the Newbery Honor Book, The Friends of American Writers Award, the Boston Globe / Horn Book Award, the Jane Addams Award, a nomination for the American Book Award, and two lifetime achievement awards: The Emily Lee Award, and The Armenian Star Award. His translations and retellings include the Asian Classic: *Monkey: A Journey to the West*. An hour-long documentary of his poetry and life by filmmaker Jim Belleau was released in 1997, and can now be seen among his Youtube appearances.

www.ingramcontent.com/pod-product-compliance
Lightning Source LLC
Chambersburg PA
CBHW032051180726
48284CB00004B/1291

* 9 7 8 1 9 4 8 7 3 0 9 3 8 *

# The Reich Without Hitler

# Volume 1

# The Falcons of Malta


ISBN: 978-1-938339-24-0
By Scott Palter with Mike Rohde
Content Assistance from: Markus Baur, Marco Pertoni

Other Assistance: Igor Bunimovich, Erik Fischer, Duane Oldsen

Editing: Jennifer Seiden Sadler

Layout, Cover and Maps: Sam Pray

Historical note – The historic July 17th promotion list has moved up to June 22nd.

Soviet moves into Romania and the Baltic states are also somewhat altered.

In the second book of this series, it will be revealed that an order regarding airships was in fact not carried out.

Free source material will be available at http://store.genreconnections.com/alternate-history-1/

# Chapter 1

0413 hours Central Euro Time [all future times are CET unless otherwise indicated],

24 June 1940

Berlin

Reinhardt Heydrich was a careful man. His house guards were handpicked for personal loyalty. The sounds of submachine gun fire as they died defending him gave him time to awaken. With the war won, it seemed Himmler no longer had need of him. However, one could die with a certain dignity. So, he had his pants on and his pistol out as the heavy thuds of the assassination squad sounded through his house up to his bedroom door. His main thought was thankfulness that his wife was away visiting family.

"Reinhardt, it's not quite what you think." That was Nebe's voice. Nebe was Kripo. Himmler wouldn't send Kripo for a liquidation mission. He and Himmler both trusted Nebe's professional competence, but it ended there. The man was a career policeman who had opportunistically joined the Nazis, not one of the glassy-eyed, blond fanatics Himmler would have sent from SS House.

"Come in slowly. Without the pistol." Heydrich was sardonically amused. Had one of the half-assed coup plots come off? If so, could he stall for time until it collapsed?

Nebe slowly entered the room after calling out first. He was in full police uniform, but had a Party armband on. He was making a point and Heydrich recognized it. "Coup in whose name?"

Nebe kept his hands in plain sight. "As I said, not what you think. The Führer is dead. Himmler's quacks seem to have poisoned him. Went into convulsions on a flight back from Paris. Pilot diverted to nearest main field. Happened to be Kesselring's HQ. Kesselring put a security lid on it. Anyway, Reichsmarschall Göring's in as Chancellor and Führer. General Beck's back. Generals Halder and Gestapo Müller are with us. Bormann, Hess, and Goebbels are dead already." Nebe stopped. He seemed to be listening for something. Heydrich listened as well. The sound was distant but clear. Artillery fire. Artillery fire in Berlin. Nebe's face lit with a frozen smile. "SS House and Party HQ. Himmler will be dead by morning. Göring wanted to settle scores with you, but I talked him around. Said you could be useful. The Air Marshal is willing to